MY WICKED WICKED WAYS

SANDRA CISNEROS

Third Woman Press
Berkeley

Some of these poems have appeared previously in *Bad Boys, Nuestro, Revista Chicano-Riqueña, Quarterly West, Prarie Voices, The Spoon River Quarterly, Mango, Third Woman, Banyan Anthology 2, Ecos, Imagine*, and *Contact II.*

Printed by Bookcrafters, Chelsea, Michigan

Manufactured in the United States of America

ISBN 0-943-21901-9
Library of Congress Catalog Card Number: 88-165489

Address inquiries to:
    Third Woman Press
    Chicano Studies
    Dwinelle Hall 3412
    University of California
    Berkeley, California 94720

First printing: December 1987
Second printing: October 1990
Third printing: March 1992

Tarde o temprano,
for Rubén

ACKNOWLEDGMENTS

Funding for completion of this manuscript was provided in part by a grant from the Illinois Arts Council, for which I am grateful. I would also like to express my gratitude to the University of Texas at Austin and the Texas Institute of Letters for their generosity and support of my work. Finally, my sincerest thanks to editor Norma Alarcón for faith and, above all, patience.

My Wicked Wicked Ways

Table of Contents

viii

1200 South/ 2100 West

I've stayed in the front yard all my life.
I want a peek at the back
Where it's rough and untended and hungry weed grows.
A girl gets sick of a rose.

—*Gwendolyn Brooks*

Velorio

You laughing Lucy
and she calls us in
your mother

Rachel me you I remember
and the living room dark
for our eyes to get used to

That was the summer Lucy remember
we played on the back
porch where rats hid under

And bad boys passed to look
and look at us and we look back
Lucy think how it was

Rachel me you
we fresh from sun and dirty
the living room pink

The paint chipped blue beneath
so bright for our eyes
to get used to and in rows and rows

The kitchen chairs facing front
where in a corner is a satin box
with a baby in it

Who is your sister Lucy
your mama not crying
saying stay pray to Jesus

That baby in a box like a valentine
and I thinking it is wrong
us in our raw red ankles

And mosquito legs
Rachel wanting to go back out again

you sticking one dirty finger in

Said cold cold the living
room pink Lucy and your hair
smelling sharp like corn

Sir James South Side

Sugar Rat the sweet-lipped one
says he will love her like no other
Genuine Forever and She—*He is insane*
Though gang love is true love
and I no jousting brother
a wild mouth is crazy and bad aim
I play the game straight
don't go looking for trouble
not capping nor the heart's high bail
no sir I say just party in peace
to all people that walk by or ride

South Sangamon

We wake up
and it's him
banging and banging
and the doorknob rattling open up.
His drunk cussing,
her name all over the hallway
and my name mixed in.
He yelling from the other side open
and she yelling from this side no.
A long time of this
and we saying nothing
just hoping he'd get tired and go.
Then the whole door shakes
like his big foot meant to break it.
Then quiet
so we figured he'd gone.
That day he punched her belly
the whole neighborhood watching
that was Tuesday.
So this time we lock it.
And just when we got those kids quiet,
and me, I shut my eyes again,
she laughing,
her cigarette lit,
just then
the big rock comes in.

Abuelito Who

Abuelito who throws coins like rain
and asks who loves him
who is dough and feathers
who is a watch and glass of water
whose hair is made of fur
is too sad to come downstairs today
who tells me in Spanish you are my diamond
who tells me in English you are my sky
whose little eyes are string
can't come out to play
sleeps in his little room all night and day
who used to laugh like the letter k
is sick
is a doorknob tied to a sour stick
is tired shut the door
doesn't live here anymore
is hiding underneath the bed
who talks to me inside my head
is blankets and spoons and big brown shoes
who snores up and down up and down up and down again
is the rain on the roof that falls like coins
asking who loves him
who loves him who?

Arturo Burro

Jacinto el pinto
Maria tortilla
Agustín es zonzo
tin tan tan

and we hide
yeah we hide
we got Arturo
inside inside
my brother
who spins his eyes

Mama says nothing
she never says nothing
Papa makes us promise to lie
3 kids we got remember it
but we got Arturo inside

He moves slow
like an elephant goes
and spits and spits
and never cries
and won't grow old
and won't grow old
my brother who spins his eyes

Mexican Hat Dance

Crash the record came down on your head.
Your were trying to dance the Mexican hat dance.
The black disc on the floor and your shiny feet
taping this way and then over that.
So you missed. So you're a lousy dancer.
Your mother, never amused by your jokes,
besides, it was her favorite record—Lucha Villa,
the lady who sings with tears in her throat,
picks it up and cracks it over your head.

Come out of that bathroom.
No, I'm never coming out!

Good Hotdogs

for Kiki

Fifty cents apiece
To eat our lunch
We'd run
Straight from school
Instead of home
Two blocks
Then the store
That smelled like steam
You ordered
Because you had the money
Two hotdogs and two pops for here
Everything on the hotdogs
Except pickle lily
Dash those hotdogs
Into buns and splash on
All that good stuff
Yellow mustard and onions
And french fries piled on top all
Rolled up in a piece of wax
Paper for us to hold hot
In our hands
Quarters on the counter
Sit down
Good hotdogs
We'd eat
Fast till there was nothing left
But salt and poppy seeds even
The little burnt tips
Of french fries
We'd eat
You humming
And me swinging my legs

Muddy Kid Comes Home

And mama complains
Mama whose motto
Is mud must remain
Mama who acts
So uppity up

Says mud can't come in
Says mud must stay put
Mama who thinks that
Mud is uncouth

Cannot remember
Can hardly recall
Mud's what I was
When I wasn't at all

But mud must remain
Or Mama complains
Mama who cannot
Remember her name

I Told Susan Reyna

I told Susan Reyna
I don't like her
because she's fat and ugly
and she wears big brassieres
and smells like chocolate candy
and comes in late each morning
with her tongue puff puffing
and her wrinkled blouse
half in half out
and who probably stole
Walter Milky's money
and never gives back pencils
just sleeps all day
while we do numbers
or all the time in a red pen
she got for her birthday
writes Susan Susan Susan
in fancy letters

The nun says
we must be kind
to everyone
or rot in fires
including Susan
who is sick
and has the fits
till she gets tired
then two boys
have to hold her legs
down and one girl her dress
and she gets to sleep all day
and wakes with crumpled hair
and spit

This
is who I told
I don't like you
because you stink

of chocolate
and menstruation
and who is sick
already 48 hours
but I don't care

Twister Hits Houston

Papa was on the front porch.
Mama was in the kitchen.
Mama was trying
to screw a lightbulb into a fixture.
Papa was watching the rain.
Mama, it's a cyclone for sure,
he shouted to his wife in the kitchen.
Papa who was sitting on his front porch
when the storm hit
said the twister ripped
the big back oak to splinter,
tossed a green sedan into his garden,
and banged the back door
like a mad cat wanting in.
Mama who was in the kitchen
said Papa saw everything,
the big oak ripped to kindling,
the green sedan land out back,
the back door slam and slam.
I missed it.
Mama was in the kitchen Papa explained.
Papa was sitting on the front porch.
That light bulb is still sitting
where I left it. Don't matter now.
Got no electricity anyway.

Curtains

Rich people don't need them.
Poor people tie theirs into fists
or draw them tight as modest brides
up to the neck.

Inside they hide bright walls.
Turquoise or lipstick pink.
Good colors in another country.
Here they can't make you forget

the dinette set that isn't paid for,
floorboards the landlord needs to fix,
raw wood, linoleum roses,
the what you wanted but didn't get.

Joe

Joe Joe's mama's baby
grown man 54 years old and lazy
Joe who is landlord and landlady
upstairs neighbor of Blanca and Benny
and let us have our Beatle fan club
under basement stairs where
waterbugs crawled out from all
over our favorite picture
of Paul McCartney

Watch out said Blanca
Watch out said Benny
Little girls beware Run away
he was the boogie man
the same Blanca saw asleep
with only underwear
and a lady's stocking on his head

He and Davy the Baby's brother
in that garage for hours
Fat cigars butts on the floor
like those waterbugs we killed
beneath our shoe And on the walls
naked lady pictures
real and not real
for Joe and Davy's brother
to look at slow

And now Joe's mama who is tired
who is a little puff of smoke
behind the screen calls Joe
out of that garage and quick
while Joe who is also tired
yells upstairs no and takes
his fat cigars and his fat nose
and his aqua car and goes
Then we don't hear

hours and hours and
meeting is adjourned until
when all will read in the papers
tomorrow how Joe who is the same
who says Yes I like go-go
and No I don't see Beatle movies
dies under a wheel
on the road to St. Charles
which everybody knows
was God's will

Traficante

for Dennis

Pink like a starfish's belly
or a newborn rat,
she hid the infected hand
for some time
before they noticed.
First the skin had been smooth
as the left hand.
Then the fence
had poked through,
a tiny slit, the mouth of a small fish.
A crispy scab had stitched it to a pucker
but this was picked on until the wound
turned a purple-pink
and gradually became swollen
and hurt to the touch.
She liked to draw the fat hand
into her sleeve,
keep it hiding there,
a fish in its cave.
Sometimes it would come out
and she would talk to it.
At school the teacher
pulled the hand out suddenly
and the child yelped.
The mother took her
to Traficante's Drugs
where the doctor had an office
behind the case of eyeglasses
all colors and different styles.
He asked to see the hand.
The fish poked out
from the cuff of a nubby sleeve,
darted back in, then was out again
and placed upon the table
beneath the bright lamp.
One finger pressed its side

and she whimpered.
The doctor took down from the shelf
the medical encyclopedia, vol.2,
and holding her by the wrist
said turn around.
Mrs. Ortiz was having a prescription filled
for Reynaldo's fever and was asking
how much when the book came down.

My Wicked Wicked Ways

Isn't a bad girl almost like a boy?

—*Maxine Hong Kingston*

My Wicked Wicked Ways

This is my father.
See? He is young.
He looks like Errol Flynn.
He is wearing a hat
that tips over one eye,
a suit that fits him good,
and baggy pants.
He is also wearing
those awful shoes,
the two-toned ones
my mother hates.

Here is my mother.
She is not crying.
She cannot look into the lens
because the sun is bright.
The woman,
the one my father knows,
is not here.
She does not come till later.

My mother will get very mad,
Her face will turn red
and she will throw one shoe.
My father will say nothing.
After a while everyone
will forget it.
Years and years will pass.
My mother will stop mentioning it.

This is me she is carrying.
I am a baby.
She does not know
I will turn out bad.

Six Brothers

In Grimm's tale *The Six Swans* a sister keeps
a six-year silence and weaves six thistle shirts
to break the spell that has changed her broth-
ers into swans. She weaves all but the left
sleeve of the final shirt, and when the brothers
are changed back into men, the youngest lacks
only his left arm and has in its place a swan's
wing.

In Spanish our name means swan.
A great past—castles maybe
or a Sahara city,
but more likely
a name that stuck
to a barefoot boy
herding the dusty flock
down the bright road.

We'll never know.
Great-grandparents might
but family likes to keep to silence—
perhaps with reason
though we don't need far back to go.
On our father's side we have a cousin,
second, but cousin nonetheless,
who shot someone, his wife I think.
And on the other hand, there's
mother's brother who shot himself.

Then there's us—
seven ways to make the name or break it.
Our father has it planned:
oldest, you're doctor,
second, administration,
me, he shrugs, you should've been reporting weather,
next, musician,
athlete,
genius,

and youngest—well,
you'll take the business over.

You six a team
keeping to the master plan,
the lovely motion of tradition.
Appearances are everything.
We live for each other's expectations.
Brothers, it is so hard to keep up with you.
I've got the bad blood in me I think,
the mad uncle, the bit of the bullet.

Ask me anything.
Six thistle shirts. Keep a vow of silence.
I'll do it. But I'm earthbound
always in my admiration.
My six brothers, graceful, strong.
Except for you, little one-winged,
finding it as difficult as me
to keep the good name clean.

Mariela

One day you forget his bitter smell
and one day you forget your shame.
You remember how your small cry
rose like a black bird from the corn,
when you picked yourself up from the earth
how the clouds moved on.

Josie Bliss

*When you die, she used to say to me, my
fears will end.
MEMOIRS*, Pablo Neruda

Explain
about the hand
the infection
raised
from some
nostalgia
a tropical dream
of Wednesdays
a bitter sorrow
like the salt
between the breasts

the palm
a lotus
a brown girl
around the neck
sleeper tell
me

the ones
you held like me
the ones who loved
your hard wrists
and belly
this

tiger circle this
knife blade
man I have no power
over

I the Woman

I
am she
of your stories
the notorious
one
leg wrapped
around
the door
bare heart
sticking
like a burr
the fault
the back street
the weakness
that's me

I'm
the Thursday
night
the poor
excuse
I am she
I'm dark
in the veins
I'm
intoxicant
I'm hip
and good skin
brass
and sharp tooth
hard lip pushed
against
the air
I'm lightbeam
no stopping me

I am
your temporary

thing
your own
mad
dancing
I am
a live
wildness
left
behind
one earring
in the car
a finger-
print
on skin
the black smoke
in your
clothes
and in
your
mouth

Something Crazy

The man with the blue hat
doesn't come back anymore.
He stopped a long time ago.
Before I got married. Before the kids came.
Nobody looks at me like that anymore.

I remember days I couldn't wait to work.
He left me big tips. He had a good smile.
But what I gave my eye for
was that moment when he'd turn around
as he was leaving
and look at me.

Oh I was crazy
for that man a long time.
Came in every day for three years.
Never said a word besides what he was having.
He'd eat and pay and just as he was leaving,
turn around.

I was young then, understand?
Nobody ever looked at me before.
I even dreamed that he might take me
to my high school dance, imagine.
Waitresses have come and gone.
I've stayed on.

The man with the blue hat
doesn't come back.
I wish he did.
I wish he did.
Just so I could say, Mister
that was quite a crush I had.

Just so I could laugh.
What I felt for him was different,
something crazy. The kind of thing
you look for all your life.

In a red-neck bar down the street

my crazy
friend Pat
boasts she can chug
one bottle of Pabst
down one swig
without even touching
teeth grip
swing and it's up in
she glugging like a watercooler
everyone watching
boy that crazy
act every time gets them
bartender runs over
says lady don't
do that again

Love Poem #1

a red flag
woman I am
all copper
chemical
and you an ax
and a bruised
thumb

unlikely
pas de deux
but just let
us wax
it's nitro
egypt
snake
museum
zoo

we are
connoisseurs
and commandoes
we are rowdy
as a drum
not shy like Narcissus
nor pale as plum

then it is I want to hymn
and hallelujah
sing sweet sweet jubilee
you my religion
and I a wicked nun

The blue dress

at the corner
over your shoulder
waving solitary small
the blue dress
bouquet in one arm
blue wind
curve of the belly
the blue dress is waving
goodbye

Five & Ten
there are flowers
and you buy her some
You want to gather
her small shoulders
in one arm like a brother
Want to tell her that you love her
You do not love her
You buy her flowers

Sunday's pass is good
till six she says
Her arms are thin
The nuns get mad she says
Her white skin
She knows the subways now
as if she were a native
The simple curve of the jaw
Someone offers his seat
You never noticed
She takes it
And her eyes are blue

The meal you paid for
you can't eat at all
She talks of towns you know
names you don't
asks if she can have

what you're not eating
She says any day now
You don't know what to say
Monday is my birthday
Her favorite color is blue

Blue as a pearl
the blue dress approaches late
You wait along the whale display
a slower gait a thinner smile
swell of the belly
ridiculously blue
The blue dress embraces you

The letter said come Sunday
Sunday is best
No men allowed
I am fine
At the museum wait
You wear your best suit
and the tie your mother gave you
You buy the ticket for your flight
Sunday at the museum
the blue dress
yes

The Poet Reflects on Her Solitary Fate

She lives alone now.
Has abandoned the brothers,
the rooms of fathers
and many mothers.

They have left her
to her own device.
Her nightmares and pianos.
She owns a lead pipe.

The stray lovers
have gone home.
The house is cold.
There is nothing on t.v.
She must write poems.

His Story

I was born under a crooked star.
So says my father.
And this perhaps explains his sorrow.

An only daughter
whom no one came for
and no one chased away.

It is an ancient fate.
A family trait we trace back
to a great aunt no one mentions.

Her sin was beauty.
She lived mistress.
Died solitary.

There is as well
the cousin with the famous
how shall I put it?
profession.

She ran off with the colonel.
And soon after,
the army payroll.

And, of course,
grandmother's mother
who died a death of voodoo.
There are others.

For instance,
my father explains,
in the Mexican papers
a girl with both my names
was arrested for audacious crimes
that began by disobeying fathers.

36

Also, and here he pauses,
the Cubano who sells him shoes
says he too knew a Sandra Cisneros
who was three times cursed a widow.

You see.
An unlucky fate is mine
to be born woman in a family of men.

Six sons, my father groans,
all home.
And one female,
gone.

Other Countries

And at times we feel
a little like exiles; a woman feels like that
when she does not live up to the image of
her required by the times, when she does
not interpret it, and hence searches for
paths, for other 'countries' where life for
her will be different from that in her own
country, in the homeland given her by her
mother's womb.

—*The Three Marias*

Letter to Ilona from the South of France

for Ilona Den Blanken Nesti

Ilona, I have been thinking
and thinking of you since I went away,
dragging you with me across the south of France
and into Spain. Then back again.

I ran away to an island off the coast,
tiny jewels of fields beneath the jewel of sky—
and lost myself one night in crumpled poppies.

Odd for such a city poet like me
to find such comfort in the dark—
I who always feared it—and yet
I loved the way it wrapped me like a skin.

All those stars, Ilona. And wind.
Field illumined by those poppies.
Yes, that was good.

I wanted to bring that back forever,
wrap it in a velvet cloth to show you.
The wind from Africa. The field of poppies.
The way my bicycle hummed the distance.

And for me, Ilona, who has never known
the liberty of darkness, who has never
let go fear, how do I explain a joy this elemental,
simple like your daughter's hand outlined in crayon.

And yet I think you understand
my first sky full of stars—
you who are a woman—
the wind from Africa, the field of poppies,

the night I let slip from my shoulders.
To wander darkness like a man, Ilona.
My heart stood up and sang.

Ladies, South of France—Vence

At 4 p.m. the promenade begins.
The wives who walk with husbands
and the ones without
who do not walk at all.

They gather like dusty birds
beneath their paisley
and polk-a-dot
and plaid and blue-checked
and yellow and plum-colored
parasols.

And in their penny-whistle French
each evening when the sunlight dims,
they sing.

December 24th, Paris—Notre Dame

The Seine runs along.
Merrily, merrily.
The river. The rain.
Water into water.

A blue umbrella fading into fog.
A child into his mother's arms.
Buttresses leaping delirious.
Wind through the vein of trees.
The rain into the river.

Tomorrow they might find a body here—
unraveled like a poem,
dissolved like wafer.
Say the body was a woman's.
Ophelia Found.
Undid the easy knot and spiraled.
Without a sound.

A year ends
merrily. Merrily
another one begins.
I go out into the street once more
The wrists so full of living.
The heart begging once again.

Beautiful Man—France

I saw a beautiful man today
at the cafe.
Very beautiful.
But I can't see
without my glasses.

So I ask the woman next to me.
Yup, she says, he's beautiful.
But I don't believe her
and go to see for myself.

She's right.
He is.

Do you speak English?
I say to the beautiful man.
A little, the beautiful man says to me.
You are beautiful, I say,
No two ways about it.
He says beautifully, Mercí.

Postcard to the Lace Man—The Old Market, Antibes

To tell the truth,
I can't remember your name.
It's those Catalán eyes
I can't let go of.

That and the memory
of an inky tea
sweetened with orange water,
the sticky perfume
of a cigarette
from Persia,
those photos of Tangiers.

I forgot to tell you.
I have a great respect
for wives.
Especially yours.

Au revoir, mon ami.
C'est la vie.
That afternoon
at the Musée Picasso—
a pretty memory and enough
for me.

Letter to Jahn Franco—Venice

You were full of stories.
Was that red jacket of yours *really*
once Bob Marley's?
The man you live with *actually*
your brother?
Those three women from Valencia
all your lovers?

It doesn't matter.
Venice was a good adventure.
Dancing through canals.
Ducking bridges from a motor boat
that sped delirious at 4 a.m.
under a laughing moon.

So I let you down.
Didn't give in and fall
under the spell of a bona fide
Venetian artist on the street,
replete with easel. A modern
Casanova—wow.

I remember that pathetic last ciao
you gave me at the railway station—
you said you felt as if
you'd bought an ice cream cone
and it had fallen to the ground
before you had a chance to taste it.

Bought.
Always that metaphor somehow or other.
And what was I
except an item not for sale.
Well.

After all, a man invests his time,
his money even,
though this was fifty-fifty.
I owed nothing.

Tell me,
one artist to another,
what does a woman owe a man,
and isn't freedom what you believe in?
Even the freedom to say no?
At least you did the night before
when we clinked our glasses to the muses
and our common god.

I don't know.
For all that talk of liberation
I still felt that seam of anger
when I danced with you
and sometimes not with you at all.

What if I hadn't gone home alone?
Say my eye had gotten tangled with another's.
Or maybe yours.
It might've happened that way.
You never know.

But to tell the truth
I think true nature rises
when the body dances.
Perhaps that's why I never
have one partner,
prefer to dance alone.

No, I won't
come to Sardinia with you.
Or even Spain.
The truth is that uncomfortable next morning
we had nothing to say to one another.
Hardly a word until we reached the station.

An ice cream cone.

In case you change your mind, you said.
I know you won't, but just in case,
I'll wait in Venice seven days.

You were right about one thing—
I didn't come back.

To Cesare, Goodbye

Cesare,
with those Medici eyes
you could go far
I said.

But you've never
been away from Tuscany
except for a cousin's wedding
in Milano.

I said come with me to Spain.

Spain you said and laughed.
Too far away—
even Rome is too expensive.

You were waiting for
that job at the post office,
a letter from an uncle
that might help.

Maybe one day
I will see you in America
I said.

Maybe
you said.
And laughed.

Ass

for David

My Michelangelo!
What Bernini could compare?
Could the Borghese estate compete?
Could the Medici's famed aesthete
produce as excellent and sweet
as this famous derriere.

Did I say derriere?
Derriere too dainty.
Buttocks much too bawdy.
Cheeks so childishly petite.
Buns, impudently funny.
Rear end smacking of collision.

Ah, misnomered beauty.
Long suffering
butt of jokes,
object of derision.
Pomegranate and apple
hath not such tempting
allure to me
as your hypnotic
anatomy.

Then
am I victim
of your spell,
bound since mine eyes
did first espy
that paradise of symmetry.

And like Pygmalion transfixed,
who sincere believed
desire could unfix
that alabaster chastity,

grieved the enchantment
of those small cruel hips—
those hard twin bones—
that house such enormous
happiness.

Trieste—Ciao to Italy

for Natale Mancari

Maybe we should've fallen in love.
Or pretended to be.
What was there to lose
except a few hours of sleep.
You needed me.

But that wasn't reason enough.
And love is no charity,
no tin cup and yellow pencils.

What did we expect?
Trieste was full of disappointments—
a town that got lucky and had the sea.
And how could I explain in raggedy Italian
I still liked you.

Maybe when your train gets into Milano
and mine to Dubrovnik, we'll perhaps regret
what didn't happen. Maybe.

But any town with a name
this sad deserves nothing
but a stoney memory.

Peaches—Six in a Tin Bowl, Sarajevo

If peaches had arms
surely they would hold one another
in their peach sleep.

And if peaches had feet
it is sure they would
nudge one another
with their soft peachy feet.

And if peaches could
they would sleep
with their dimpled head
on the other's
each to each.

Like you and me.

And sleep and sleep.

Hydra Night—House on Fire

When houses burn here
you just watch.

There is nothing
but the sea
for irony.

Cinders wild as flies.
Rooster crowing day too early.
Night illumined. Moonless sky.

I worked with others
dragging furniture outdoors—
books, tables, lamps—
to save what could be saved.

Water drizzled from a skinny hose.
Buckets passed from
hand to hand to hand.

Somebody cursed in Greek.
A neighbor gave me her sweater,
asked if I was cold.

First the grape arbor came down.
And then the windows spoke.
We watched until the roof
sighed twice, then died.
Then one by one went home
to dream of fire.

Hydra Coming Down in Rain

I'm not certain
but I imagine even
mountains melt.

In Hydra
they come down
in rain

and down
on cobbled
steps
inside your shoes
unless your boots
are rubber
red.

Bleed
from lemon trees,
white-washed walls,
wooden shutters,
gravel,
bougainvillea,
clay tile roof,
pomegranate,
copper gutter,
slippery flagstones,
fresh donkey shit,
and jasmine flowers.

Down and down
until the mountain
meets the port

and spills
into
the sea.

Fishing Calamari by Moon

for A. Stavrou

At the bullfights as a child
I always cheered for the bull,
that underdog of underdogs,
destined to lose, and I tell you
this, Andoni, so you'll understand,

though we are miles from bullrings.
The Greek moon a lovely thing
to look at above our boat.
We are an international crew tonight.
Greek sea, *African Queen,* you, me.

But I am sad. Probably the only
foolish fisherman to cry
because we've caught a calamari.
You didn't tell me how

their skins turn black
as sorrow. How they suck the air
in dying, a single terrifying cry
terrible as tin.

You will cook it in oil,
You will slice it and serve it
for our lunch tomorrow.
Endaxi—okay.

But tonight my heart
goes out to the survivors,
to the ones who get away.
To all underdogs everywhere,
bravo, Andoni. Olé.

Moon in Hydra

Women fled.
Tired of the myth
they had to live.
They no longer wait
for their Theseus
to rescue, then
abandon them.

Instead,
they take
the first boat out
to Athens.
Live alone.
No longer Hydra women
bound to stone.

Smoke rises
from the Athens shore,
and some say
it's the fumes of autos,
motor scooters,
factory pollution.

But I think
it's an ancient rage.
Women who grew tired
beneath the weight of years
that would not buckle,
break nor bend.

One Last Poem for Richard

December 24th and we're through again.
This time for good I know because I didn't
throw you out—and anyway we waved.

No shoes. No angry doors.
We folded clothes and went
our separate ways.

You left behind that flannel shirt
of yours I liked but remembered to take
your toothbrush. Where are you tonight?

Richard, it's Christmas eve again
and old ghosts come back home.
I'm sitting by the Christmas tree
wondering where did we go wrong.

Okay, we didn't work, and all
memories to tell the truth aren't good.
But sometimes there were good times.
Love was good. I loved your crooked sleep
beside me and never dreamed afraid.

There should be stars for great wars
like ours. There ought to be awards
and plenty of champagne for the survivors.

After all the years of degradations,
the several holidays of failure,
there should be something
to commemorate the pain.

Someday we'll forget that great Brazil disaster.
Till then, Richard, I wish you well.
I wish you love affairs and plenty of hot water,
and women kinder than I treated you.
I forget the reasons, but I loved you once,
remember?

58

Maybe in this season, drunk
and sentimental, I'm willing to admit
a part of me, crazed and kamikaze,
ripe for anarchy, loves still.

For a Southern Man

Bill, I don't do laundry
and I don't believe in love.
I believe in bricks.
And broken windshields.
And maybe my fist.
But you're safe to take
the road this one time, buddy.
I'm getting old.

I've learned two things.
To let go
clean as kite string.
And to never wash a man's clothes.
These are my rules.

I want to learn to say
see you next Tuesday.
Then drive away.
The windshield whole.
The rearview empty of regrets.
Though now and then
there are exceptions.

What I remember of
a room at dusk
and how your bones
continued from a single strand.
Finger knuckle spine.

To love too much to leave behind
a neon sign in northern Georgia,
pink and blinking THE PINES.

That laundromat in Landis
famous for the way
it makes you sad.

The blond waitress at Jay's Diner,
counting passing cars,
dreaming of the one that got away.

The Rodrigo Poems

This is the Hour of Lead—
Remembered, if outlived,
as Freezing persons, recollect the Snow—
First—Chill—then Stupor—then the letting go—

—Emily Dickinson

A woman cutting celery

is savage
because a car door slams.
But he does not come home.

Miles after thoughts
have turned from worry,
have turned to rage,
a car door slams.

And she is cutting
celery and more celery,
but no familiar stumble

of the key. Nor
crooked tug and coy
apology. No blurred kiss
to comfort this cruel

hour and quit those
sometime fears to sleep. Surely
love has strayed before.

Love has come and love has gone
and love has been away
before but ultimately
stays. It must be

the errant lover of the girl
across the way who arrives
at such an independent hour,

whose rude feet
startle gravel beyond the borders
of begonias asleep under the back
porch light. Not here.

A thin blond vein
rises from the corner of her jaw
like a crack in a porcelain plate.

A car door slams.
But he does not come home.
This is how the story begins.

Sensuality Plunging Barefoot Into Thorns

You're sick.
So I bring over my television set—
(it's okay I hardly ever watch it)—
soup,
cards,
a few books.

You answer the door
in pajamas,
fuzzy slippers,
a robe
two-sizes-too-big
(a gift from your last wife)—
ridiculous.

I don't take off my coat.
I mean to drop the things and go.
But just as I'm tugging the door,
you sneeze

and pull like a magician
from your sleeve—
a handkerchief.
Red.
Extraordinary.
Loud as timbales.

Already it begins,
all the miles home—
a slow smoke without warning.

In a few weeks
all you'll have to do is phone.

By then
the handkerchief
will have done its harm.

Valparaiso

you said
last night
we are a zoo

and you
were right
we are
blue

fur and the open night!

an animal dance
on cue
and continued
your cigarette

what are you thinking?

here
is the mise en scene
a man
a woman
a cigarette

silhouettes
against the landscape
of sheet and pillow
a pretty

setting
one might think
and why

should one know better?

correction
this is a case
of mutual

hunger

of polite
request and courteous
take

and love
that rude religion
is neither

diffident
correct
nor safe

ours
is a narcissistic
yearning
yours

a city

mine
my necessary
fame

no

do not
mistake
this myth
for love—

that
is a different
kind
of burning

I understand it as a kiss

but not a kiss. This
gesture, this burning.
But from an origin
furthest from the heart.

I recognize this
is for me, and yet
I sense I make no
difference. I know

if we say love
we speak of many things.
You mean the Buenos Aires moon,
the blond streetlamps,
the dance you danced.

But I know it as the wrist,
a shoe, a bruise,
a bone, a stick.

For All Tuesday Travelers

I am the middle-of-the-week wife.
The back-door sneak.
I wake the next-door neighbors
who wonder at who arrives so late,
departs so early.

Who yearn to know
the luxury of love delivered.
Love that comes and goes
without the ache,
without the labor.

It is a good life.
I would not trade it
for another wife's.

I who am the topic
of the Wednesday morning chatter.
Who in her lone society
politely sips the breakfast given her.

Correctly travels with a toothbrush,
her own comb. Says *thank you,
please, goodbye,* and runs along.

No Mercy

Your wives left
without a trace
Both of them

They plucked
their long hair
from the kitchen sink
did not forget the ring
nor the domestic combs
Not one stray stocking
did they leave

Not a fingerprint
nor a subscription
to a magazine

They fled

Gathered their feathers
and bobby pins and string
Left nothing

Took their towels
and their initials
one child
expensive shoes

and vamoosed

Without a clue

You must've said
something cruel
You must've done
something mean
for women to gather

all of their things

The World Without Rodrigo

moves
at a slender pace
does not mind to hesitate
undoes one button
exhales with grace
walks does not run
hums

Rodrigo Returns to the Land and Linen Celebrates

puffed with air
the muslin and satin
the fitted and flat
the dizzy percale
and spun cotton
billowing and snapping
sun-plumpt and flapping
everywhere! everywhere!

Beatrice

No doubt you are still
waiting endlessly
for your Beatrice.
Sudden on the steps
of a bridge where
as a boy you waited.
Hopeless even then.

Kiss me.
I am an odd geometry
of elbows and skin,
a lopsided symmetry of sin
and virtue. And you.

I can feel your eyes
burning over the horizon
of my shoulders.

Rodrigo de Barro

You are red clay
    and river water, Rodrigo.
Simple enough.

This is your skin.

And from what
    my hands and mouth
have memorized

I could shape the myth
    of bones
into the flutter of collar,
    the arias
of ladders and spirals.

Collect the necessary
    snail shells
and bits of yellow stone.

Crumble them in my palm.
    Here
are your eyes.

I know by heart the salt
    and smoke
elixir of your neck and fingers—

my new intoxicant, my bitter liquor!

And could I tether a thousand
    bees together,
I would create the zoo of dreams
    that you dream each night.

But where to find enough
    ignited Alexandrias,
an explosion of heliotropes
    and roses,

all the mutinies and revolutions,
    the Hannibals
and Nebuchadnezzars,
    an army of
Russian bears,
    25 dancing Lippizans,
and one rare white Bengali,
    to burn
    in the veins,
to march without end,
    a dagger and
a silk heart. Oh my cruel
    Bonaparte,
my loveliest Caesar.

Rodrigo in the Dark

Rodrigo, your red tie
slips from the neck
with a serious sigh.
The shirt of many buttons,
the woolen trousers, and
the handsome shoes
forget their reasons for formality
and take their eager liberty—
delinquent and lovely without you.

I like the rudeness of the moon
that lets me look at you
without permission,
the slender bones tossed
careless as tulip stems,
the bouquet of shoulders,
the dip and hollow of the skin.

Without your uniform of havoc
you are simply a man
like any other.
No longer white tiger,
my rival and keeper.

Good night, my Bengali.
This is my pirate hour.
Count one, two, three—
Rodrigo snoring beside me.

Then it is I can begin again,
to speak of love without apology,
with only the black mustache listening,
the beard cynical and stiff.

The So-and-So's

Your other women arc well-behaved.
Your magnolias and Simones.
Those with the fine brave skin like moon
and limbs of violin and bones like roses.
They bloom nocturnal and are done
with narry a clue behind them.
Narry a clue. Save one or two.

Here is the evidence of them.
Occasionally the plum print
of a mouth on porcelain.
And here the strands of mermaids
discovered on the bathtub shores.
And now and again, tangled in
the linen—love's smell—
musky, unmistakable,
terrible as tin.

But love is nouveau.
Love is liberal as a general
and allows. Love with no say so
in these matters, no X nor claim nor title,
shuts one wicked eye and courteously
abides.

I cannot out
with such civility.
I don't know how to
go—not mute as snow—
without my dust and clatter.
I am no so-and-so.

I who arrived deliberate as Tuesday
without my hat and shoes
with one rude black tatoo
and purpose thick as pumpkin.

One day I'll dangle
from your neck, public as a jewel.
One day I'll write my name on everything

as certain as a trail of bread.
I'll leave my scent of smoke.
I'll paint my wrists.
You'll see. You'll see.
I will not out so easily.

I was here. As loud as trumpet.
As real as pebble in the shoe.
A tiger tooth. A definite voodoo.

Let me bequeath
a single pomegranate seed,
a tell-tale clue.
I want to be like you. A who.

And let them bleed.

Monsieur Mon Ami

And now, my pretty one,
you have announced
perfunctorily and promptly,
you will be offing in the morning.

You say it audibly.
You say it calmly
so as not to alarm me.
I understand the words
and yet hardly comprehend.

Where to and when with no warning?
Paris? Marakesh? Sao Paolo?
Where, love, and how without me?

You pack the lovely clothes.
The handsome shoes move
back and forth across the wooden floor.
Back and forth. Ignore me.

I trace arabesques in the table dust.
Say nothing. Not a sound, in fact.
A good sport.

Bon voyage, I say,
and kiss each cheek goodbye.

Though all the drive home
the thick heart bleeds.
An ulcer.
A toothache.
A plum.

Something begins its slow hiss.
Hysterical. High-pitched.

The brain clicks like a gun.

Drought

Because of pride
I don't phone.

Not me.

On the contrary
I place the telephone
over there.

Against the wall.

At the far end of the room.

And stare at it for days
like cigarettes.

Oh I'm greedy like a drowned lady.
I want and want my grief—
each cell must have its fill—
and I want more of it.

It's worse at night.
Sky tilts.
All the dark pours in like sand—
a gun against the brain.
Hopeless.

I dial.

Ring once . . .
twice . . . finally!
It's you.

Although the voice is little—
a bee inside a bell.

Hello; it's me.
Then silence like a seam.

How are you?
Silence again.

Fine, fine, I mumble, fine,
unraveling like string.

And then I can't hear myself
above the racket in the brain.

By Way of Explanation

There is—
I suppose—
a bit of
Madagascar
in me
I never mention.

And somehow
Amazons
have escaped
your rapt
attention.

The nose
is strictly
Egypt
for your
information.

The heart
a cruel
white circle—
pure Bengali.

Here are the knees
you claim are yours—
devout Moroccans.

The breasts
to your surprise,
Gaugin's Papeete.

Pale moon of belly—
Andalusian!

The hands—
twin comedies
from Pago Pago.

The eyes—
bituminous
Tierra del Fuego.

Odd womb.
Embalmed.
Quintana Röö.

Amé, Amo, Amaré

i.

What you said was
I do not love you.
Simply.

Not once.
Not ever.
Not now.
Never.

Then you took me
home with you
because it was time
to undress me.

There was a moon.
All the numb ride there
it followed me
and grinned.

There was the house.
Same as before.
Same rattle of the door.
Same sigh of burgundy.

You took me in.
Just like the other nights.
Same tug. Same urgency.

Made love,
just as a lover does.
Kissed me.

ii.

I don't remember that night.
That is, I don't remember
the words you used precisely.

I'm not sure who
asked and who answered.
Whether I shut

my eyes or furled
myself tight as a rose,
I don't know.

Only that gossip moon
already mentioned—
wisecracking, whispering.

Here is the little flag of news
that lodged itself into the brain.
How the truth finally came.

Isn't it funny?
When you tug me beside you
I dissolve like a ribbon of snow.

And you tell me.
The words clearer than ether,
purer than poem.

A wife, a wife, a wife.
The woman you love and who loves you.
All your life.

iii.

Christ! Don't act
as if you didn't know—
under your breath.

Years later over coffee one day
you'll confess—What went on
in your head that night
to make you so strange.

Because I've folded myself up
like a bird. I've folded
one wing across one breast,
the other, across the heart.
Stiff as jute. Mute as an Egyptian.

There.
I've ruined the evening.
I've ruined everything.

I put my stockings on.
My green green dress.
(Funny I remember that detail—
the green green dress.)

And worse,
you have to take me home.
The long cold drive.
The big black car.
The wide front seat.

You sitting far at the other side
like a man at the wrong
end of a telescope.

The moon winks.
I'm a simp I think.
But I'm wrong.
I know what I am.

Men Asleep

I have known those who sleep like a Ulysses
beautiful in their 20-year weariness.

And those who would drown
themselves each night like lost sons.

And those who could not let go of
the leather loops of their love,
their work never done.

And those who go room into room into room,
who shut themselves like doors,
who would not let me in.

New Year's Eve

I saw your wife tonight.

No Athena. No Medea.
No Adelita nor Malintzín.

From what I could observe
she is a woman risen from a rib
like any other—
two eyes, two breasts, one uterus.

She did not arrive
wearing raiments of gold
on a barge from the Nubian Nile.

No Botticelli pearl is she
riding the crest of a wave
on a pretty half shell.

She did not trophy
serpents in each upraised fist
mighty as a priestess.

She neither graced her
walk with flowered skirts
and balanced basket,

nor stand Carmenesque,
hands on hips, and thrust
her haughty laughter out.

She did not sling
a rifle upon her back,
nor a child across her breasts.

Fire did not issue from her gaze
and no music from her lips.

Her hands were clean.
Her forehead modest, serene.

How did I fail to understand?
A female, like any common female.

For a common male.

14 de julio

Today, *catorce de julio,*
a man kissed a woman in the rain.
On the corner of Independencia y Cinco de Mayo.
A man kissed a woman.

Because it is Friday.
Because no one has to go to work tomorrow.
Because, in direct opposition to Church and State,
a man kissed a woman
oblivious to the consequence of sorrow.

A man kisses a woman unashamed,
within a universe of two I'm certain.
Beside the sea of taxicabs on Cinco de Mayo.
In front of an open-air statue.
On an intersection busy with tourists and children.
Every day little miracles like this occur.

A man kisses a woman in the rain
and I am envious of that simple affirmation.
I who timidly took and timidly gave—
you who never admitted a public grace.
We of the half-dark who were unbrave.

Tantas Cosas Asustan, Tantas

Tantas cosas asustan. Tantas.
Los muertos y los vivos.

Lo que la oscuridad no nos permite ver
y lo que nos permite.

Pasos sobre un patio
tanto como el silencio.

Y cosas simples.
Aritmética. La renta.

El infinito también asusta.
Números. El cielo.
Dioses que siempre fueron y serán.
La inmortalidad.

¿Cuál es peor?
Estar siempre sola,
o estar con alguien para siempre.

Y el finito aterroriza.
Nuestras vidas por ejemplo

El amor asusta.
Igual la luna y los generales.
Y pesan mucho.

No uno por uno.
Pero todos juntos.
Como una lata de canicas.

La felicidad, al contrario,
es otro asunto.
Tiene que ver con papalotes.